LORD OF THE MORNING

Lord of the *Morning*

PRAYERS FOR THE START OF THE DAY

FRANK TOPPING

DIMENSIONS
FOR LIVING
NASHVILLE

LORD OF THE MORNING:
PRAYERS FOR THE START OF THE DAY

First British edition published 1977

Dimensions for Living edition published 2002
This edition published by arrangement with The Lutterworth Press

This book is printed on recycled, acid-free, elemental-chlorine–free paper.

Library of Congress Cataloging in Publication Data has been requested.

ISBN 0-687-04502-9

02 03 04 05 06 07 08 09 10 11—10 9 8 7 6 5 4 3 2 1

MANUFACTURED IN THE UNITED STATES OF AMERICA

To June

CONTENTS

JOY

In this morning hour
I want a fresh chance
To start again.
I don't want to waste the minutes and hours
That have been given to me.
I want to be alive
To every experience,
In conversation,
In the mundane tasks of this day.
In moments of relaxation
I want to find joy in living.
Lord of the morning, help me.

Lord, help me to enjoy
The common things of my everyday life.
I often find myself saying that
Nothing happened today,
When in fact the ordinary events of my life
Make a rich pattern,

But they are so familiar
I hardly notice them,
Things like cups of tea and coffee
And meals shared with friends and colleagues;
Or listening to favorite family stories
That we have heard and told so often.
Lord of life, help me
To recognize the joy of simple things.
There are so many familiar mileposts
That I stop and lean on, every day,
So familiar,
That I don't realize how much
I enjoy their comfort and support;
Like the smile of the woman
Behind the shop counter,
The therapy of being lost
In a good book,
Or a radio play,
Or my favorite music.
The days are rich in pleasing moments
That I take for granted.
Lord of life, help me to realize
The joy of living.

When I come to the end of this day,
Help me to remember
The big problems that turned out
To be little ones,
And the things I worried about

That never happened.
Lord of laughter and joy,
Help me to see,
To experience
And to treasure
Every good moment.
Lord of the morning,
Lord of life,
Lord of light, help me.

A NEW BEGINNING

Lord of the morning,
I'm trying to forgive myself
For the mistakes I've made.
There are too many "if onlys" in my life.
If only I had been more thoughtful,
If only I had been kinder.
I blame myself for so many things
Yet I cannot turn back the clock.
I have to live today,
Even with my self-inflicted wounds.
Lord, help me to live with myself.

Lord, in this hour
I need to be able to forgive myself
But I also need to be able to forgive others,
To *really* forgive.
How often have I gone through the motions of
    forgiveness,
Only to let my mind dwell on the wrong
    remembered?

And even to talk about the people who have failed
   me,
That is not forgiveness.
I know that I cannot erase experiences from my
   mind,
But even bitter words heal
And though the scars remain
They can grow faint and be forgotten.
Lord of life,
Help me to forgive, and to be forgiven.
It would be so good to be able to start again,
With a clean slate;
To make a new beginning,
To be born again.
I want the old, muddled, muddied me to die.
I want new life.
Here am I, sinner and sinned against.
Is there a love that will cancel my sins?
Have I the love that will cancel
The pain caused by friends?
I know that it is possible,
I know that love can bring the dying back to life.
Lord, fill me with the love that you offer,
So that I may know that I am forgiven
And be so full of your love
That it will spill over into the lives
Of all the people I live and work with.
Lord of life, help me.

In this hour, Lord,
Help me to look forward
Rather than to sigh over past events.
Help me to see the good that *can* be done
The caring that *can* be offered
The love that *can* be given.
While I mope about myself
There are people waiting for the kindness I can give.
Lord, help me to give, to share,
To start again a renewed life.
Lord of the morning,
Forgive me and help me to start again.

PANIC!

Lord of the morning,
I don't know why
But I sometimes feel a panic
Rising inside me.
I know it is irrational
Yet some days I am afraid.
The letter that falls on the doormat,
The sudden ringing of the telephone
Fills me with fear.
I'd like to escape, to run away
But there's nowhere to run
Except to you.

Lord of life,
Why do I anticipate the worst
When time and time again
The worst never happens?
Even when it does, life goes on
And every day comes to an end.

Lord, help me to overcome my fears
In this brief moment of reflection
Calm my mind
Help me to relax
Let your comforting Spirit
Enter into me
And fill me with peace.
In this hour
Open my eyes to all the things
That you have given
That help, support, and lift
Troubled minds.
Let me find joy
In the beauty of a single flower,
A branch of a tree,
Or the vast embracing sky.
Help me to hear the love
That lies in the ordinary words
Of friends and family,
To remember the words of
Guidance that wait for me
In the rarely opened Bible or prayer book.
I know your love will lift me up.
Help me to trust you.

Lord, help me to be thankful
That yesterday's problems have passed.
Help me to measure today
Not by the difficulties I *might* meet

But by the good things the day will bring.
Help me to know that *this* day
Will be full of gifts.
Give me the knowledge that no matter what
  happens
Today, or any day,
Nothing can separate me
From you and your love.
Lord of the morning, help me.

PURPOSE

In this morning light
The same old questions fill my mind
Like, what am I doing with my life?
What do I really believe in?
Is there a purpose for humanity, for me?
Lord, I believe, help my unbelief.

In this morning light
I look for meaning.
What is it I want out of life?
What do I hope for?
What can I achieve?
What should I be doing with the days, the years
That have been given to me?
I want to be useful.
I want to be needed.
I want to love and be loved.
Lord of the morning, help me.
Lord of the morning,

I find it so hard
To see what things really matter,
To see what is important in my life.
There are so many distractions,
So many demands,
Responsibilities, worries—
There is just so much to cope with.
And I do worry
Even though I know I am worrying
About the wrong things.

Lord of the morning,
Give me this day
The wisdom to recognize what things are important
And what things are not.
Show me what to do
With the time and the talents you have given me.
Give me faith, give me hope,
Help me to trust in your guidance
All the days of my life.
Lord of the morning, help me.

OTHER PEOPLE'S PROBLEMS

In this hour
The world clamors for my attention
And I don't want to hear.
I don't like listening to the news
Or reading the newspapers,
They depress me somehow.
I suppose I don't really want to hear about
Other people's problems, yet
I know I cannot ignore my neighbors.
Lord of life, help me.

Lord, why am I afraid
Of being involved in the world around me?
I know the answer really:
It's because I cannot face
The demands that come
From so many who need help;
The poor who need my money,
The sorrowing who need my comfort,

The lonely who need my time.
Lord of life, give me the strength
To listen to the needs of others,
To give what I can, whether it's help or time.

Lord of life,
The world about me is changing—
Different needs in different places.
I hear myself saying,
"How different things are from when I was young."
Things are different, I am different,
Older, if not much wiser.
But you never change.
From age to age your love continues,
Your love is constant.
I know this
Yet I give and love so little.
Lord of love, help me.

Lord,
Forgive me for ignoring the needs of others
And for missing opportunities of giving and serving.
If I see the truth, dimly,
If I stumble as a beginner in faith,
If I am, only now, beginning to wake up
To the fact of your love,
Help me, help me to see you,
To love you and to follow you,
Lord of the morning,
Help me.

BEING ALONE

In this morning hour
I am alone
With millions throughout the world who are alone.
Some are solitary in a kitchen
Or a studio.
Others are in cars in traffic jams,
Or in the cab of a truck on a road.
Sometimes it is good to be alone,
But loneliness hurts.
Lord of life, help me.

Lord of life,
This loneliness is a passing thing.
Soon I will be with others,
Companions, friends, family,
And I can hide from myself
In their company.
But there is a deep aloneness
That is hard to live with

When the soul seems empty.
Lord of life, fill my emptiness.

Lord, loneliness comes in many forms.
For some it is the emptiness of bereavement,
Widow, widower, or orphan,
Divorced or separated by circumstance.
Lord, you know what it is to be alone, to feel
     deserted.
Help me not to wallow in self-pity,
Fill my emptiness with your spirit
Until the cold core within me
Is warmed by your love.
Lord of life, help me.

In this hour
I ask to be given someone to love;
I don't want a hand to hold
But someone to love by caring.
This day must be full of people to love,
Even if only for a little time.
Help me to lift others up.
Take over my life so that when I am alone
I will not be lonely
For you will live in me.
Lord of life, come now
And help me.

MONEY WORRY

In this morning light
I seem to be obsessed
With worries about money.
I have hardly noticed
If the sky is cloudy
Or if the sun is shining.
I have eaten breakfast absentmindedly.
I am finding it hard to concentrate
Like someone lost in a maze.
Every corner I turn
Brings me up against a dead end
Or another bill.
Lord of the morning,
I am in your presence,
I need your help;
Calm my mind.
Lord, have I got things out of proportion again?
Why do I let things get the best of me?
When I think of my family

And how much they mean to me,
When I think of the love I receive,
How stupid it is
To be depressed by a telephone bill.
When I think of your creation,
The sky is just as endless,
The sea as wide and fathomless
As it was yesterday
And will be tomorrow.
Deep down I know that the world will not end
Because of a rate increase.
Lord of the morning, help me.

Lord, help me to keep my balance,
Keep alive my sense of humor,
Help me to laugh at myself
And my ridiculous fears,
Lift me out of my maze of petty worries,
Relax my fretful mind
With its small concerns
And show me the largeness of life
That I might be grateful
In the knowledge that I am rich
In basic fundamental things.
I am alive, I love and I am loved—
What are a few bills?
Lord of the morning,
Thank you.

DISCONTENT

In this morning light
I feel the grayness of winter.
The things about me
Seem tired and worn;
There is a sameness about the pattern
Of my life
And it's hard to avoid
The tedium of my daily routine.
There are times when familiar faces
Are a comfort.
But there are times when I long
To start again,
To see new faces
To live in a different place,
To find a new way of life.
Lord, I know that there are many
Who would gladly exchange places with me,
And I feel guilty

Because I know I undervalue the work I have been
    given.
I am sometimes deliberately blind
To the richness of workaday friendship.
I know that I waste
Valuable hours of relaxation;
I let them slip through my fingers.
Lord of the morning, help me.

Lord, lift me up
With your spirit,
The spirit which gives purpose to my life,
The spirit which brings joy
Into ordinary conversation,
The spirit which brings peace of mind
In the midst of tension and fatigue,
The spirit that turns colleagues
Into friends,
The spirit that lifts familiar works and action
Into gestures and signs of love,
The spirit that renews all things,
Even me.
Lord of the morning,
Spirit of life and love, help me.

FRIENDSHIP

In this hour
I remember the face of a friend,
A friend that I haven't seen for some time
And I would like to see again.
There are so many friends I have lost touch with
And it would be so easy
To pick up a phone, or send a card.
Real friendship is too precious
To forget or neglect.

Lord, I need friends
But I wonder what kind of a friend
I am to others.
I know I am guilty of using other people
Even people I care about deeply.
Help me to be warm in greeting people.
Help me to give, to give some love
And friendship to all the people I shall meet this day.
Lord of the morning, help me.

I am often selfish with my friends.
I want them to listen to *me*,
To *my* problems, and I only
Half listen to them.
Lord of life, forgive me.

Lord of life,
Help me to be a friend,
A trustworthy friend;
To be able to defend
When others gossip or criticize.
Greater love has no one
Than to lay down one's life for a friend.
Sometimes I am not able even to lay aside
Five minutes for those who need my time.
Lord, help me to realize both the gift
And the responsibility of friendship.

Lord,
Help me to really look
At the people that I pass fleetingly every day,
The people on the fringe of my life.
Help me not to be enclosed
Within the inner circle of my own friends
But to offer friendship
To those who find it difficult
To make friends.
Lord of the morning, help me.

GOD BE IN MY HEAD

In this hour
Somewhere in the world
People will be meeting on buses and trains
In shops, factories, and offices.
Some will meet only for a few fleeting moments,
Others will spend most of the day together.
I may meet people who will cheer me,
Make me smile or maybe annoy me.
Lord of the morning, help me.
In the hours ahead
I may bring the warmth of friendship to some,
Others I may irritate and anger.
Lord, life is too short for bitterness,
For quarreling, or for hurtful gossip.
Yet sometimes it is hard to think kindly
About those I share my days with.
Lord of life, help me.
Through the hours of this day
I may say things that I will regret,

Things that will hurt or cause bitterness,
Yet in doing this
I hurt myself,
Spoil my own day.
Sometimes I am my own worst enemy.
In the way I think of people,
Talk to people,
Work with people,
Lord of life, help me.

Lord of life, throughout this day
Take over my mind,
My words,
My actions,
My life.

God be in my head,
And in my understanding;
God be in mine eyes,
And in my looking;
God be in my mouth,
And in my speaking;
God be in my heart,
And in my thinking;
God be at mine end, and at my departing.
Amen.

ANGER

In this morning light
I'm trying to control
A feeling of anger,
Anger that is not simply in my brain
But eats its way into my very being.
I've tried to dismiss it,
And for a time I do;
Then a word, or a face
Flits across my mind
And the anger surges back.
I want to lash out
But I know that if I do
Things will be worse.
Anger is never satisfied;
It feeds on harsh words and thoughts.

I know that I should be big enough
To cope with gossiping tongues,
Innuendo, insulting words,

But I cannot ignore the fact
That they upset me, hurt me.
I don't want to be caught up
In the futility of anger,
The destructiveness of anger,
The loss of control that returns
Hurt for hurt,
The wild use of words as weapons
That break friendships
And damage lives.
Lord of the morning, help me.

Lord, I know what I should do
But doing it is another matter.
I always think of what I should have said
Afterward
When it's too late.
It's hard to offer love in the face
Of jealousy or spite,
To resist anger,
To be a peacemaker
When popular voices are on the attack.
Lord, at least help me
Not to be the source
Of anger in others.
Throughout this day
Be with me—in my mind,
In my eyes,
And on my lips.

RECONCILIATION

In this hour
There is new opportunity,
Opportunity to start again,
To forget old failures,
Old mistakes.
But where can I start
With so many mistakes to mend?
Quarrels between friends,
Thoughtless words that hurt,
Pride that makes reconciliation hard.
Lord of the morning, help me.

In this hour
Help me to make a fresh start
In my marriage,
To love through all the moments
Of joy and sadness
In good times and bad
For richer or for poorer

In sickness and in health
Till death us do part.
Help me, Lord,
To love and cherish
Throughout my life.
Teach me the way
Of gentleness and care.
Help me to remove the barriers
That separate
Family, friends,
Brothers, sisters,
Sons and daughters.
Teach me the way of reconciliation
That being reconciled to those about me
I might be reconciled to you.

Lord,
Give me the ability
To say that I'm sorry
When I have been wrong.
Give me the words
That will heal the wounds
That I have caused in quarreling.
Give me the wisdom to understand
Those who disagree with me.
Give me the grace
To accept another's point of view.

Lord,
Fill me with your spirit

That I might, where there is hatred, give love;
Where there is injury, pardon;
Where there is doubt, faith;
Where there is despair, hope;
Where there is darkness, light;
Where there is sadness, joy.
Lord of life, help me.

TOO BUSY
TO LOVE

In this morning light
I seem to be hurrying
Into the day.
I see about me
Those who share my life,
Yet in the hustle
For bathroom, breakfast, and bus,
They only merit a glance
Or a brief word.
Eye on the clock
Toast in my hand
It takes too much time
To say, "I love you."
Lord, in the morning rush, help me.
Lord of the morning,
Moments like these are rare,
Moments when I stop to ask myself,
"What am I hurrying for?"
The days are so busy,

Working, earning, getting,
That I almost have no time for living,
No time to enjoy the company
Of my wife and children.
I waste precious moments,
Moments that could live with me
For the rest of the day,
Moments when we touch or
There's a meeting of eyes.
Lord, help me to be still with them
At least one moment today.

Lord, in this moment of stillness
Help me to remember that I am loved
Even though I don't deserve it.
I am loved by family and friends
And amazingly, I am loved by you.

Lord of the morning,
Help me to stop rushing.
I can't love my family in a hurry.
Help me to take time off
To love.

INTERCESSION

In this morning light
The streets are busy
With nameless people on their way to work.
There are faces everywhere,
Behind newspapers on trains,
Looking down from the windows
Of buses,
Peering through the windshields
Of cars.
And in each mind
There is a question that needs an answer
Or a problem that must be faced
Or a decision to be made.
Millions of people
In cities, towns, and villages,
Every one is different
And yet somehow
Every one of them is me.
Lord of the morning, help us.

As this morning light
Falls in shafts
Through different windows,
It reveals a hospital ward,
Nurses, doctors, patients.
Lord, give them the strength
They need for this day.

As doors open in schools,
Factories, and offices,
Men, women, and children
Begin a day
That might make many demands,
Teachers in their relationships
With children,
Children with new ideas
And things to learn.
In industry, on shop floors,
In homes, and at office desks
We will struggle with the business of the day.
Lord, help us.

In this morning light
My problems seem so difficult
That it is hard to find words
To express them.
Lord of the morning,
Why do I seek for words
When you know the things

That are in my mind?
All I have to do
Is to say,
"Lord, look at me."
Take the confusion out of my head,
Calm the panic
That seems to rise in my chest.
Lord, take over.
Guide me in the things
I will say and do today.
Help me in the decisions I must make.
Reassure me that your support
Is always available to me,
And that I have but to ask
And you will provide the strength
That will carry me through
Whatever this day might bring.
I am asking for your help now.
Lord of the morning, help me.

FORGIVENESS

In this morning hour
The world listens to itself,
To the things that people like us are doing
To each other.
We shake our heads and wonder
What the world is coming to
And whether it is possible
To be forgiven for what we have done
To the world and to ourselves.
Lord of life, help us.

Forgiveness is what we need
For the grudges we hold,
For the thoughts we think,
For the words we say,
For the things we do
That hurt and disfigure
Our fellows and ourselves.
Forgiveness is what we need.

Forgiveness is what we need;
Forgiveness for our created dust bowls,
For earth ravaged by greed,
Forgiveness for the misuse of beauty,
For the desecration of what is rich and lovely
In exchange for what is cheap and tawdry,
For guns and bombs,
For the savage destruction
That we have wreaked for centuries;
Lord of life, help us.

You, Lord, are the God of mercy,
The forgiving God,
The giver of peace,
And peace of mind is what we need,
The peace that is harmony with our fellows,
Harmony with creation and the creator,
The peace that comes from mutual forgiveness—
Peace in our homes,
Peace in our hearts,
Peace in the world.

But God so loved the world
That he gave his only begotten son
That whosoever believes in him
Should not perish but have eternal life.
And we who are crippled by sin,
Deformed by selfishness,
Can, if we listen, hear the voice that says,
"Rise up: your sins are forgiven you."

WHO—ME?

In this morning light
As I try to bring some order
Into my mind
I sometimes catch a glimpse
Of the obvious.
In a brief moment of insight
I see myself as others see me.
Not for long—I shut it out
Because I do not want to see
The unloving face that I so often show
To my wife, my children,
To the people I meet in passing
Every morning.

Lord of the morning,
What blinds me
To my own shortcomings?
What incredible arrogance
Makes me see all my faults
As virtues?

I see myself as "a bit of a perfectionist"
When others see me
As impatient and conceited.
I see myself as being modest
Or humble about my achievements
While others hear me boasting.
I like to see myself doing things
For other people's good
When in fact I'm mainly concerned
About what is good for me.
I think I am a loving person
But really I am in love
With the idea of love
Not the life of love.

Love is patient and kind;
Love is not jealous or boastful;
It is not arrogant or rude.
Love does not insist on its own way;
It is not irritable or resentful;
It does not rejoice at wrong,
But rejoices in the right.
Love bears all things,
Believes all things,
Hopes all things,
Endures all things.
Love never ends. (RSV)
Lord of the morning,
Help me to see love, to know love,
And to live in love.

HEARING AIDS
AND WALKING CANES

In this morning light
The young rush to school and to work
And the elderly watch them go;
Those old eyes that have loved,
That have closed tight in the agony and ecstasy
Of childbirth;
Eyes that have shared the pain and joy
Of family life;
Eyes that have looked long into the hollow pit
Of grief.

So often I talk to the elderly as if
They were children.
I give them Christmas presents of chocolates
And bars of scented soap.
I am impatient with the frailty of age,
Their slowness, their deafness, their aching bones;
Heroes with hearing aids and walking canes,
Smelling of pipe tobacco

And lapsing into the stillness
Of minds lost in memories of the past.
These are the people who lived through wars
For me,
Suffered for me, wept for me,
Nursed me, loved me.
How dare I mutter
"Silly old thing"
Of a woman who may have given more to humankind
Than I can even imagine.
How dare I dismiss
As a "doddering old fool"
The huffing, puffing man
Who survived torpedoed ships for me,
Lay in trenches,
Dug coal mines
For me.
Lord of the morning, forgive me.

Lord, this day
Take from me
The arrogance of the modern mind.
Help me to understand,
Give me the patience to hear
The old and oft-repeated stories.
Help me to learn from their experience,
To value the wisdom garnered
From the harvests of many years.
Give me the eyes to see

The beauty of age,
To learn that love and life
Are not confined to youth
But reach out to eternity.
Lord of the morning, help me.

FEELING TIRED

In this morning light
The world shakes itself awake
Like a great shaggy dog
And prepares to meet another day.
Cups and saucers rattle
And millions of homes
Are filled with the morning smell of toast.
In various places machines have started.
In factories and on farms.
People board buses and trains,
Letters are opened
And telephones start to ring.
I too should be coming alive
But somehow I feel so tired.
Lord of the morning, help me.

Lord,
Why is it that so often
I start the day feeling tired?

Sometimes I know that the reason
Is simply lack of sleep,
Going to bed too late,
Staying up talking into the wee hours,
And that's my fault.
But sometimes I feel tired even after
A good night's sleep.
Is it because I don't want to face work
And responsibility?
Lord of the morning,
Give me the strength
To face the tasks of this day.

In this morning light
Some of the things I have to do
Seem to loom large before me,
And I carry the prospect of work
Like a heavy burden weighing me down
Even before I begin.
Yet by this evening many of today's
Difficulties will have passed.
Maybe they will prove to have been
Far less arduous than I imagined.
The thought of a problem
So often turns out to be worse
Than the problem itself.
Lord, lift my spirit,
Give me energy and a sense of humor
Throughout the hours of this day.
Lord of the morning, help me.

DAILY WORK

In this morning light
I'm thinking about my daily work.
I sometimes wonder
How I came to have my present job
Or why I earn my living
In my particular way.
Should I be doing something else with my life?
Should I be looking for something new,
Something better, or ought I to be content,
Grateful for employment
When many have no work at all?
Lord of the morning,
During this working day, guide me.

Lord, over the years I have been caught up in the
    race
For something better.
Perhaps this is the time to stop,
To stop racing ahead, to take stock.

If I have learned my trade,
If I am competent in my work
Perhaps I should stay where I am
And try to improve what I do.
Lord, is that common sense
Or simply cowardice?

Lord, throughout the hours of the day
Help me to appreciate
The work I have been given to do.
If I have talents,
Help me to use them.
Let me not waste my gifts by neglecting them
Or through craving the gifts of others.
Help me to be courageous
In decisions about the use of my time and energy
At work and at home.
Lord of the morning, help me.

BUSY DOING NOTHING

In this morning light
I feel regret
For the time that has slipped through my fingers.
Days pass so quickly.
I feel busy
Yet I seem to have done nothing.
I start a day with good intentions
But I keep putting things off.
Suddenly the day is nearly spent
And I am telling myself,
"I feel tired, I'll do it tomorrow."
Sometimes I suspect
I am putting off living.
Lord of the morning, help me.

Lord, sometimes
I am like someone walking up
And down saying,
"I'm busy, I'm very busy,

I've got so many things to do.
I haven't got time for the thing that I'm doing now."
But how long does it take
To live now?
How long does it take
To notice somebody?
How long does it take
To send a card to say,
"Thinking of you"?
How long does it take
To look at a flower,
To smile, and say a prayer?
Lord of the morning, help me.

Lord, help me to work out
The things I have to do today.
There are probably only
One or two really important things.
Give me the courage
To tackle those things first
And then show me
That I do have time
To listen,
Time for kindness,
Time for laughter,
Time for love.
Lord of the morning,
Help me not to be
Too busy to live.

TOMORROW AND ITS NEEDS

In this morning light
Lies the day ahead.
All my apprehensions and fears,
My hopes and longings
Rise up once more.
Sometimes I am almost overwhelmed
At the thought of starting again.
Little things bother me:
What clothes to wear,
What bus or train to catch.
How will I manage today,
With the bigger things,
With people and events?
Lord of the morning, help me.

In this morning light
Are the faces of those I will meet
At the newsstand,
In travel,
At work,

Over coffee and lunch.
And I am anxious—for success,
To please, to be loved—self-centered.
It's hard to turn around,
To let others please me,
To love others because *they*
Need loving,
Not because of what's in it for me.
Lord of the day, help me.

In this morning light
I look ahead
As always,
Always to the future,
Never now.
Always the next problem
Instead of this moment of peace.
It's hard to enjoy *now, today,*
Because it's not just the next problem
But tomorrow's problems
Which sometimes never happen.

Lord, help me not to let my life
Revolve about the possible trials of tomorrow.
Give me the courage to resist the temptations
That will stand before me today
So that today may have moments
When I may be counted worthy
Of the Lord of my hours, my minutes,
My life.
Lord of the morning, help me.

MY WORLD

In this morning light
My sleep-laden eyes are reluctant
To meet the hurly-burly of the world.
Lord, help me to get my world into perspective.
What is my world?
My home? My family? My friends?
All of them I suppose.
The people who support me every day
By their presence,
Who share my problems,
Argue with me, eat with me,
Criticize me, laugh with me,
Love me—these are my family,
My world.
Lord, I know that I have a responsibility
To a bigger world;
But help me not to forget how much
I need those who share the ordinary things of every
    day.

And do not let me pass by those who are lonely,
Because of shyness, or age, or some disability.
Lord, help me to be grateful
For the people I call "family"
And help me to be open
To anyone who wants to share some time
With me today.

Lord of the morning,
My small world
Is only a fraction of a bigger world.
Help me to remember
The responsibilities that I have to brothers and sisters
From different races, creeds, and countries;
Brothers and sisters that I have never met
But who are affected by how I live,
By the money I earn, or spend, or give,
Who suffer because of my apathy.
And let me not forget, that they are my brothers and
   sisters
Because you are the Father of the human family.
Lord of the morning, help me.

BEING ALIVE

In this morning light
I am trying to see
What day it is.
Sometimes I seem to lose a day,
And it's a bit frightening
When I can't remember where the day went
Or what happened to the week.
And birthdays come so fast
That I have to work out how old I am.
Lord of the morning,
I don't want my life to trickle away
Like water on sand.
I don't want to waste this day;
I want to live it. Help me.

Lord of the morning,
The days that are lost
Are usually the days

When I have forgotten to stop and speak to you
In prayer,
When the hours and minutes
Have been so busy
That you have been crowded out of my life.
These are the lost days.
It's strange
But I only live my life
When I'm prepared to give it away.
The only days I keep
Are the days I am willing
To give to you.
It's a curious paradox.
I want to live
Yet I have to let *me* die
Before I can start living.
Lord of the morning, help me.

In this morning light
There is peace.
It is the peace of your presence.
In this morning light
There is sensitivity
Because of your Spirit.
In this morning light
There is power, strength, life.
It is the life that you give.

Lord, help me to give this day to you
So that I might really live.

Help me to say when things are difficult,
"Lord, this day is your day
And I belong to you."
Lord of the morning,
Help me to live.

I WISH I HADN'T DONE THAT

In this morning light
My conscience is nagging me.
There is something I have to put right, today.
Yesterday I lost my temper
With someone I love.
It wasn't simply anger,
I lost my temper, lost control,
Allowed frustration and weariness
To burst out in a flood
Of stupid, venomous words;
And this morning the bitterness
Of the hurt I inflicted is still with me.
Lord of the morning, help me.
Lord, I know that I can make excuses,
Add up all the pressures of the day,
Of the week, and say
It was just the last straw,
I couldn't help it.
But that wouldn't be true,

I wouldn't have indulged
In that uncontrollable rage
With my employer, or people I wanted to impress.
No, I had to do it to someone
Who loves me
Because deep down inside
I knew that I would still be loved
Even as you love me,
In spite of my weaknesses.

Lord of the morning,
I know that one of the privileges
Of being loved
Is to be able to let off steam
In the presence of those I love.
I know that the release
Of pent-up feelings
Can be a cleansing process,
But help me not to exploit love;
Help me in recognizing the love
That embraces me
To be changed by that love
To give love in return
This day.
Lord of the morning, help me.

A DAY
TO REMEMBER

In this morning light
The faces of my family
Smile at me from a photograph
And I find myself smiling back.
A fleeting moment of happiness
Trapped on a film
Bringing me happiness now.
At this moment I can hear them
Moving about the house,
Preparing for another day.
Today there will be difficulties and problems,
Maybe we will argue, as people do.
But today, Lord,
Let there be moments of happiness.
In this morning light
I remember an act of kindness,
A gesture of love from a small child.
I remember laughing
Until the tears ran down our faces;

I remember the excitement,
The shouting, the rocking of the boat
When we landed our first fish.
I remember Christmas trees
And birthday parties,
Sunny days on the beach,
Wet days tramping over hills.
Lord of the morning,
Help me to remember these moments
With gratitude as I go about
The ordinary things of today.

Lord of the morning,
If happiness is sharing,
Loving, giving, understanding,
Help me to share the good things of this day.
Help me to be loving
And thoughtful with family and friends.
Help me to be generous in giving
Time and attention.
Help me to be understanding
When things go wrong
So that this day will be a day of love,
A day to remember.
Lord of the morning, help me.

CHILDREN

In this hour
All over the world
Mothers and fathers
Are thinking about
Their children
And worrying about them.
How are they getting on at school,
With their friends, with their work;
And after school
In their leisure?
What will they do?
How will they mature?
What sort of people will they become?
What will they do with their lives?
You have given us the gift of children,
Lord, guide us, to say and do the right
Things for them,
To be near them when they want us,
To love them, no matter what they may do.
Lord of the morning, help us.

In this hour
Schoolteachers prepare lessons for our children,
Work out schedules
Plan particular lessons
For particular children
Good children, sad children, happy children,
Awkward children, funny children—
Our children.
Together, parent and teacher,
We will influence them
These children,
How they think, speak, and act.
These are the days
In which we will lay the foundations
Of their lives,
Surrounding them with the things that matter:
Love, laughter, and joy,
Even bitterness, anger, and sorrow.
Lord of life, help us.

Lord,
Help us to be patient
With our children,
To give them time
When they need it,
To listen to their views
However much they may differ from ours.
Help us in our conversations together
That we may always trust each other.

As our children search for knowledge
Help us to learn with them.

Lord of life,
As we try to help and guide our children,
We realize how much
We need help and guidance ourselves.
We call upon you, as our Father,
And ask for the help of your spirit.
It was said,
"If you know how to give
Good gifts to your children,
How much more will the heavenly Father
Give the Holy Spirit
To those who ask him."
Lord, fill us with your spirit
For our sake
And for the sake of our children.

NEW YEAR

In this morning light
The old year is dying;
Even now the troubles of last year
Are fading into the past to be forgotten,
Yet there is so much to be remembered with
   gratitude.
In this coming year
I'd like to be able to sort out my life,
To throw away yesterday's mistakes
And keep the good things.
Yet I need yesterday's mistakes.

A new year is coming
And fresh hope;
I was never any good at making resolutions,
Perhaps I made too many.
I can't count the things I was *going* to do,
Or stop doing, or give up.
But I'm reluctant to give up anything.

I cling to the things I want,
Forgetting that fragile gifts
Held in a possessive grip usually break.
Lord, help me not to cling so fiercely
To the things I claim as mine
When even the breath I breathe is yours.
Lord of the morning,
Help me to give back the life I owe to you.

In this morning light
Give me courage to offer this year
And everything in it to you.
The things I may enjoy
Or the things I may suffer,
The hours in which I may be used
Or *not* used by you.
Let me from this day
Put my whole life into your hands—
Triumphs and failures,
Laughter and tears,
They are all at your disposal.
From this minute
Let me be no longer my own,
But yours.
Lord of the morning, help me.

EPILOGUE:
THE VOYAGE OF
THE *MILLER*

*This poem was written one winter while sailing on the
North Sea in a schooner called the* Malcolm Miller.

That day when evening came, he said to his disciples,
"Let us go over to the other side." Leaving the crowd
behind, they took him along, just as he was, in the boat.
There were also other boats with him. A furious squall
came up, and the waves broke over the boat, so that it
was nearly swamped. Jesus was in the stern, sleeping on a
cushion. (Mark 4:35-38*a* NIV)

Was it ever quiet?
Were we ever still?
Were all our days a
Continuous struggle
For mastery of the storm?
Gusts of passion drove us from youth,
Love was tempestuous
And the gentle softness of our years

Wounded deeply;
Scars healed and hardened us,
Taught us, and turned us
Into shellbacks
Surviving in a sea of fears.

Was it ever quiet?
Were we ever still
As we made our passage
From ignorance to knowledge,
Still for long enough
To see the stars before us,
To feel the tide,
To plot a course,
However rough and ready:
Or did we hurl ourselves
Against the breakers,
Blind within the foam,
Clasping hands with those about us,
Struggling for a foothold
On slipping, shifting, shingle stone?

A bitter brine washed us then,
A wet and cold reality
That cooled the ecstasy
Of experience.
And here,
Aloft in the arms
Of the *Miller's* rigging,

Over a gray-green sea,
I search the horizon
For the elusive stillness
That I long for, yearn for,
Hope for,
A moment of seeing quietness
In my head.

But it's never quiet here,
In the mind,
Not in this vast storehouse
Of all our days,
Of images, voices, laughter,
Of pain's intensity;
Not with an army of experiences
Tramping through the brain.
Even in our therapeutic sleep
Doors open and shut.
In the labyrinth of memory
There are signposts,
Symbols of the event.
A hand, a smile, a face,
A tree with snow-laden leaves
And we slip and slide
On a cerebral trip
To childhood.

Not what you would call quiet,
This crowded playground

Of shouting ideas,
Jumping, running thoughts,
And questions
Playing hopscotch
On the cobbles of conscience.
All our days
From that first, blind kicking
Exit from the womb,
And earlier,
When ear was pressed to belly
To feel and hear
The jerk of embryonic life,
And before that,
When did the molding start?
When did we hear
The voice of our mothers?
Where did we begin?
Who am I?

How brief
The furious storms
That tossed that adolescent sea;
How short-lived
The righteous anger
That drifts astern
In the wake of age.
There was no quietness there,
No stillness worth remembering,
Just fitful prayers
That filled the occasional lull.

The zealous vows of puberty
Scarce die on the wind
When away on the port beam
Another zephyr is sighted,
A shadowy ripple on the surface of the sea,
Moving swiftly, inexorably, toward us;
Followed by a gray-black
Impenetrable mass
That will soon engulf the ship,
And then—she strikes!
We fight to shorten sail,
Heeled hard over
Bows slice through waves
And crash into rollers,
Churning up a wide spreading patch
Of frothing water.
We clutch at shroud and stay,
Bend our heads
Against the shrieking, fearful wind
And in spite of all,
It is grand, grand,
This struggle for survival,
Grand to realize,
To learn, to know the strength
Of muscle and sinew,
Thought and deed.

This is what we came for,
To live to the brim,

To fight the battle,
To plunge into careers,
Marriage, children, property,
Laughter, tears, pain, and death.

Here is the great storm,
Life itself.
Sails tear, timbers split,
Head and hands and feet
Are wounded,
Yet still we try to stem the storm.
The ship is filling
And we must bail and pump
Till our backs ache,
For this ship is the only one we have,
This voyage is the only one we make,
And this power that drives us
Is the majesty that drives the sea.

The sea is full of people
People who struggle and weep,
People who triumph and laugh,
People who suffer and despair.
For some the days and nights are harsh
Filled with frightful cacophony;
For some there is music
That brings sense
To the madness of the maelstrom.

But who tunes the ears
That hear the sounds
That spirits make?
What notes pierce the traffic roar,
The din of markets, money, and men?
Why this carpenter,
This fisherman, this dentist,
This lawyer, farmer, teacher, priest?
Why him, why her, why me
To hear the irresistible sound
Of that small voice?
How comes the deafness
Of those who do not hear?
Are lives more wicked
Or time more wasted?
Which office worker is measurably
More good than his fellow?
Which steeplejack is nearer to God?
Which baker molds pastry
With a holier hand?
Do they choose
Or are they chosen
To hear the whisper
That never dies?

And the waves beat into the boat
So that the boat was already filling,
But he was in the stern, asleep
On the cushion.

And now it is evening
And the day is far spent,
Tired and weary
We are ready to admit defeat.
We are broken, beaten
And fearful of death.
Yet can it be
That he who drives the sea
Sails with us?
Has he shared
The storm and all its alarms
And now sleeps in the stern
Without worry, without fear?
Who is he who sleeps in the
Face of fury?
Can this be the one who has power
Over the storm?
Can this be the one who can
Still the waves,
Who has power over life itself?
We have tried to sail
Against the wind
On each and every day
In our own strength,
In youth and maturity,
Yet throughout those years
Has he been with us?
With us in the storm,
Waiting for us to turn to him,

Waiting to be asked
To still the waves.

Lord,
Forgive me for living my life
As if you were not present.
For trusting in my own strength
And not yours.
Teach me to trust you
Especially when the journey
Seems difficult and hard.
Give me peace
That cannot be disturbed
By the fiercest storm.
Give me the knowledge
That no matter how many problems
May strew the way ahead
You who have the power
To still the storm
Can bring strength and stillness
Into my life.